2486

2/86

2486

D1306727

2486

FORESTS
and
JUNGLES

Troll Associates

FORESTS
and
JUNGLES

by Rae Bains
Illustrated by Joel Snyder

Troll Associates

Library of Congress Cataloging in Publication Data

Bains, Rae.
  Forests and jungles.

  Summary: Explains briefly the location characteristics
of forests, rain forests and jungles and describes the
interrelationship of the plants and animals that live in
them.
    1. Forest ecology—Juvenile literature. 2. Rain
forest ecology—Juvenile literature. 3. Jungle ecology—
Juvenile literature. [1. Forest ecology. 2. Rain
forest ecology. 3. Jungle ecology. 4. Ecology]
I. Snyder, Joel, ill. II. Title.
QH541.5.F6B27   1985   574.5'2642   84-8641
ISBN 0-8167-0312-4 (lib. bdg.)
ISBN 0-8167-0313-2 (pbk.)

In the heart of the forest, it is cool and shadowy. Through the leafy branches of the tall trees, thin beams of sunlight reach down to the forest floor. The ground is soft and spongy, covered with a blanket of dead, brown leaves...leaves that fell last year, two years ago, and even before then. The silence of the forest is broken by the flutelike notes of a songbird. Branches rattle and creak as a squirrel leaps from tree to tree.

In the hot tropical places of the world, there are forests of a different kind. There, the air is warm and wet all the time, and the trees are never leafless. It is a world that is eternally green.

The tall trees block out the sunlight, leaving the soft, wet forest floor in deep shade. Just a few vines, bushes, and wildflowers can grow here. This is the tropical rain forest.

At the edges of the tropical rain forest, and along open places such as rivers and streams, more sunlight reaches the ground. There, the undergrowth of vines and ferns, shrubs, tall grasses, and young trees is tangled and thick. This kind of tropical forest is called a jungle.

About one third of the dry land on Earth is covered by forest. The largest forests are in the Soviet Union and the South American country of Brazil. The forests in the Soviet Union are temperate ones, like those in North America.

Some of these forests contain mostly conifers, or evergreen trees, such as spruce and pine. The seeds of these trees are grown in tough, woody cones. Most conifers are softwood trees.

Other temperate forests contain a mixture of conifers and deciduous trees. Deciduous trees, such as oak and maple, shed their leaves in the autumn and grow new ones the next spring. Most deciduous trees are hardwood trees.

In a deciduous forest there are usually a number of different kinds of trees growing in one area. But in an evergreen forest, there is usually just one kind of tree in each section of the forest.

11

The forests of Brazil, as well as those of
other hot places in the world, are rain
forests. Rain forests are filled with a rich
variety of trees and other plants. These trees

are not conifers, yet their leaves remain green throughout the year. In one section of a rain forest, there may be fifty or more different kinds of trees growing side by side.

If you were to walk through a tropical rain forest, you would find many different kinds of plants clinging to the trees. Some of these plants might be either parasites or air plants.

The parasites, such as numerous species of fungi, steal water and minerals from the trees. The air plants, such as some orchids and mosses, attach themselves to the trees, but they take water and minerals directly from the air or from the ground.

Some air plants are called stranglers. At first, the stranglers take their food and water from the air. Then, as they grow, they send down roots that steal the food and water from the trees on which they live. Finally, stranglers surround the host trees and kill them.

Many different kinds of insects, birds, snakes, and large and small animals live in the jungle and rain forest. A naturalist once counted all the living things he saw in less than one hour as he walked through a South American jungle. There were more than six hundred creatures, over half of them insects.

He saw flies, butterflies, beetles, grasshoppers, bees, wasps, ants, mosquitoes, and spiders. He counted one hundred twenty-eight different birds—large and small, and of all imaginable colors.

And these were only the creatures he actually *saw.* Out of sight, high above and all around him, there were monkeys, lizards, all kinds of rodents, and jungle cats.

The constantly green, lush growth of the tropical rain forest is made possible by a great deal of rain. It rains here nearly every day. If you measured the total rainfall in a year, it would be higher than the head of any human being.

Yet for all this rain, tropical jungles and rain forests do not have very much fertile soil. The plants grow so fast all year long that they use up all the minerals and other nutrients in the soil.

Forest soil is usually much richer in cooler climates, where plants do not grow all year long. During the nongrowing seasons, fallen leaves and branches decay, returning minerals and other nutrients to the soil. This decaying process is helped by rain and snow.

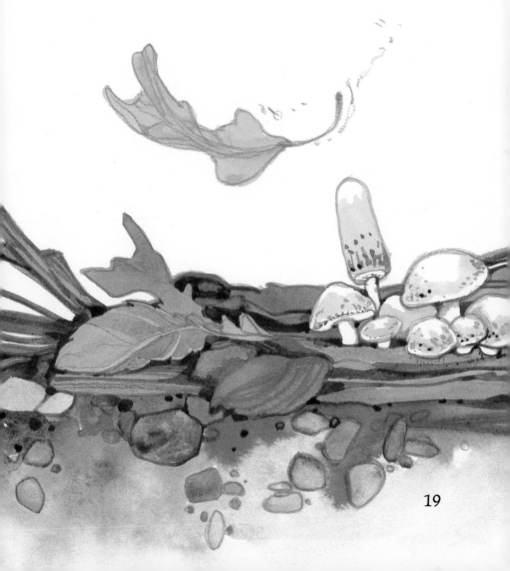

During the growing season, rain is vital to the health of the forest. In fact, forests cannot exist without enough rainfall. If the total annual rainfall in a temperate forest came down all at once, you would be standing in water up to your thighs!

For a forest to grow, there must be at least three months when the temperature is above freezing. For this reason, you won't find forests at the tops of high mountains or in the regions of the far north. In these places, even though there may be enough moisture and good soil, the growing season is just too short for forests to exist.

Forests are important in many ways. The wood of their trees is used for lumber, for fuel, and for manufacturing paper, furniture, and numerous chemical products.

Forests help prevent erosion and floods by soaking up rain and melted snow. Without these huge, natural "blotters," the water would quickly wash away precious topsoil and cause floods in low-lying areas.

A healthy forest is a beautiful world made up of several different "layers." The topmost layer is called the *canopy.* It is made up of the topmost leaves of the tallest trees and acts like a thick green roof over the forest.

In some forests, the canopy is so thick that it lets through very little sunlight. In other forests, the canopy is more like a lacy web that lets some of the sunlight filter down to the forest floor, far below.

Photosynthesis—the process by which green plants make food—cannot take place without sunlight. So most of the food that is made in the forest is made in the canopy, where there is the most sunlight.

The canopy is also the layer of the forest where some insects, birds, and small climbing animals gather to feed. But because the canopy is exposed to strong winds and rain, as well as sunlight, not many creatures live at this uppermost level.

Below the canopy is the level called the *understory*. It is home for a wide variety of birds and other small animals. The trees of the understory may be smaller, younger specimens of the trees that make up the canopy. Or they may be species of trees that grow well in the shade, such as dogwood and hornbeam.

Below the understory is the level known as the *shrub layer*. Here you will find blueberry bushes, mountain laurels, spice bushes, and other shrubs. These make perfect homes and sources of food for such small animals as deer mice and chipmunks, and for birds such as grosbeaks and grouse.

At the *herb level*, just above the forest floor, there are wildflowers and grasses, ferns, mosses, mushrooms, and tiny seedlings. In forests where the canopy allows a lot of sunlight to penetrate, this level is rich and green. When there is less sunlight, there are fewer plants here.

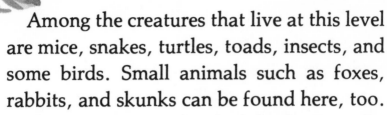

Among the creatures that live at this level are mice, snakes, turtles, toads, insects, and some birds. Small animals such as foxes, rabbits, and skunks can be found here, too.

The very bottom level of the forest is the *forest floor*. The forest floor is covered with dead leaves, flower petals, seeds, twigs,

branches, and the remains of animals, birds, and insects. All of this matter is food for the earthworms, insects, and bacteria that live in the soil. They help to break down the dead matter so that it can enrich the soil and enable new plants to grow in the forest.

Every year the forest grows and changes. Even after a fire rips through and devastates a mighty stand of oaks, life goes on. In place of the oaks, young pine seedlings take root. They grow strong, slender branches that reach for the blue sky above.

After some years, the slow-growing oaks begin to appear again. More years go by and the sturdier oaks reach above the pine trees, taking back the land. Again they make a green canopy of oak leaves over the forest floor. And in their midst live the insects, birds, and animals. In this way, the life of the forest goes on and on.